Money Matters!

WRITTEN BY NIKKI TATE

Acknowledgments

The publisher would like to thank the following for their kind permission to reproduce their photographs: (Key: b-bottom; c-center; l-left; r-right; t-top) **123RF.com:** Aliaksei Hintau 20cr (banana), belchonock 6br, damedeeso 27br (dog), homestudio 30tc, indigolotos 27cl (shovel), Ivonne Wierink 27tc (dishes), jarp5 27tl (broom), Kheng Ho Toh 25tr, Kittiphat Inthonprasit 27bc (tools), Nikita Sobolkov 27tr (Watering), picsfive 27c (garbage), Tetiana Vitsenko 28, Zerbor 8tl, zigzagmtart 6cl; **Alamy Images:** Blue Jean Images 29, Bubbles Photolibrary 26bl, D. Hurst 27cl (rake), DonSmith 23br, Finnbarr Webster 17br, Gunter Marx 8c, Jeff J Daly 12c, Justin Kase z03z 16-17b, MARKA 11br, Nik Wheeler / Danita Delimont 9tl, Picture Partners 13t, Radius Images 18c, Simon Critchley 12b, Thomas Cockrem 9br, Vincent de Vries 23tl, Werli Francois 7cr, Zuma Press Inc. 11t; **Getty Images:** DeAgostini 10bl, Eric LAFFORGUE / Gamma-Rapho 5t, GERARDO GOMEZ / AFP 15c, SHAH MARAI / AFP 7b, SSPL 10r, View Stock 14b; **Imagemore Co., Ltd:** 5b; **Imagestate Media:** John Foxx Collection 24cr; **PhotoDisc:** Jules Frazier 20tr; **Shutterstock.com:** Africa Studio 25b, Angel_Vasilev77 4tl, Anna Hoychuk 31b, dibrova 4bl, Dmitrij Skorobogatov 25tl, Elena Elisseeva 21t, fritz16 22b, Jason Batterham 19t, K.Miri Photography 24bl, Marie C Fields. 18-19, monticello 20c (bread), stable 20cl (eggs, eggs), wavebreakmedia 17tl

Cover images: *Front:* **Shutterstock.com:** Anna Hoychuk; *Back:* **Shutterstock.com:** dibrova

All other images © Pearson Education

Every effort has been made to trace the copyright holders and we apologise in advance for any unintentional omissions. We would be pleased to insert the appropriate acknowledgement in any subsequent edition of this publication.

PEARSON

ISBN-13: 978-0-328-83281-1
ISBN-10: 0-328-83281-2

6 7   18 17 16

Contents

Welcome to the World of Money   4

Let's Trade   6

What's It Worth?   10

Glittery Gold   12

Making Paper Money   14

Banks and Money   16

Borrowing Money   18

How Much Is That Loaf of Bread?   20

How Happy Is Your Country?   22

Meet Some Young Entrepreneurs   24

Pocket Money   26

Budgeting   28

Save It   30

Glossary and Index   32

Welcome to the World of Money

Money is a part of everyday life. People earn money from their jobs. Sometimes people are given money as a gift. We use money to pay for things we need. We use it to buy things we want. We can save money or we can spend it.

There are many different types of money. Coins and bills are called cash.

Read on to learn about money. Find out about different types of money. Find out how we use it. Learn to make smart choices about saving and spending.

On special occasions, children in China receive red envelopes. The envelopes contain money.

Let's Trade

We spend money on food to eat. But what would happen if we didn't have money? If you had eggs and your neighbor had apples, you could trade. Trading means *swapping* or *exchanging*. Sometimes we exchange money for goods. Sometimes we exchange goods for goods.

Eggs and apples are goods.

Cash Cows

Cows provide meat, milk, cheese, and yogurt. This means cows are valuable. For centuries, cattle were traded for other goods.

Markets are places where people buy and sell goods.

Trading Today

Kyle MacDonald of Canada traded a paper clip for a fish-shaped pen. He traded the pen for a doorknob. He kept trading until someone gave him a movie role. He used the money from the movie role to buy a house!

This giant red paper clip is outside Kyle's house. It reminds him of his first trade.

Currency

Money can take many forms. Currency is money that is used in a certain place or country. We can exchange currency for goods.

Yap people used to use giant stone money. It is still used today for special transactions such as land sales.

These people are from the Yap Islands in the Pacific Ocean.

Did You Know?

These items have all been used as currency in the past:
- ✓ shells
- ✓ blankets
- ✓ goats
- ✓ rice grains
- ✓ cacao seeds
- ✓ salt
- ✓ squirrel skins
- ✓ rings

These are glass trade beads. In the past, they were a form of currency in Africa.

What's It Worth?

Who decides whether a shell or a piece of paper is valuable? Money has value because we all agree it has value. Banks, governments, and citizens all must agree that money is worth a certain amount.

Did You Know?
Some of the first-ever coins were made in ancient China. The spade coins (above) were made to look like tools. The coins with holes (left) are easy to string together and carry.

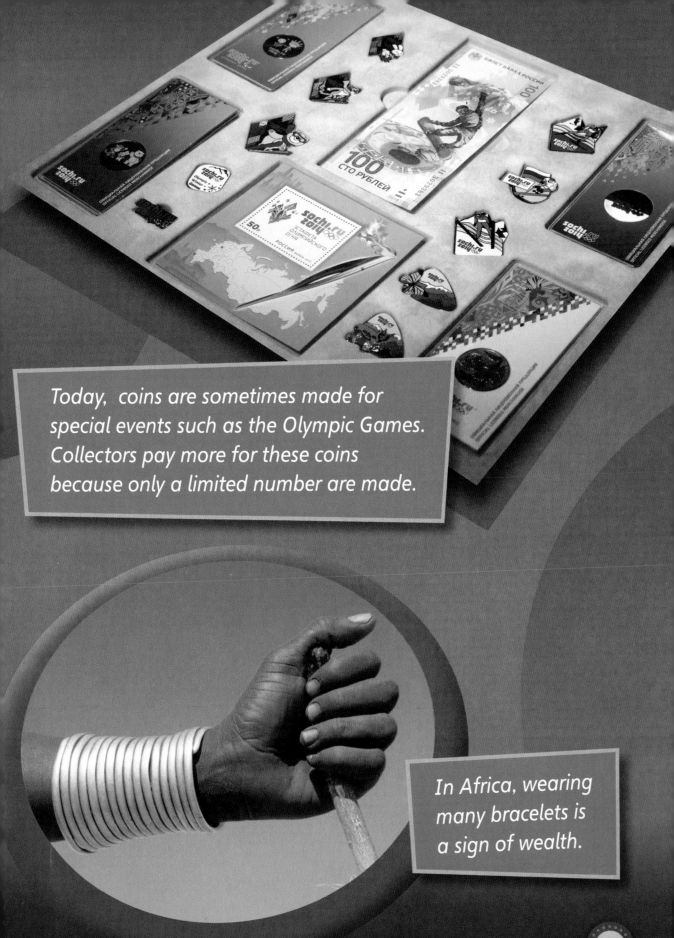

Today, coins are sometimes made for special events such as the Olympic Games. Collectors pay more for these coins because only a limited number are made.

In Africa, wearing many bracelets is a sign of wealth.

Glittery Gold

Gold is a precious metal. There is only a limited amount of it on Earth. People shape gold into coins, bars, and jewelry.

Today, people can pan for gold for fun.

Gold Rush!

A gold rush happens when people hear gold has been found. People rush to search for the gold. The people living near the gold often become rich. They build hotels and shops for gold miners and make lots of money. One of the last North American gold rushes happened along the Klondike River in 1896.

Making Paper Money

Paper money was invented in China. At first people thought it was strange. How could paper be exchanged for a chicken? Eventually people got used to it. Bills are light and easier to put in your pocket than a cow! In time, paper money became ordinary.

Did You Know?
Ancient Chinese laws made it illegal to refuse to accept paper money. Anyone who argued was killed!

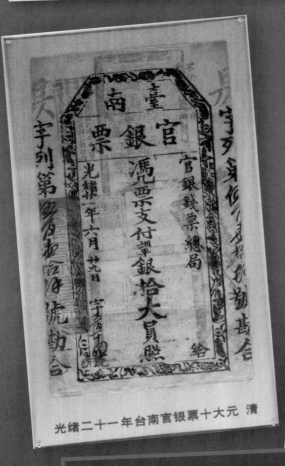

光绪二十一年台南官银票十大元 清

Ancient Chinese paper money

咸丰四年甘肃司钞五百文 清

Fake Cash!

Criminals sometimes copy official money. If there is too much fake money around, people become cautious. They don't know if the money they have is real or fake! They stop trusting cash.

Fake money is called counterfeit money.

What Do You Think?

Why is it a crime to make fake money?

Banks and Money

Every day, things are bought and sold. It is hard to keep track of everybody's purchases. Banks help us to do this. They store, track, and lend money worldwide.

A bank is a safe place to keep your money.

Today, most people use cash only for small purchases. People often use debit and credit cards to pay for goods. These cards are used for electronic transfers. Banks and shops use computers to keep track of the money.

Armored trucks move cash around.

Borrowing Money

A credit card lets people borrow money without visiting the bank. The money must be paid back to the bank each month. If not, the bank can charge extra fees on the money that has been borrowed.

People often shop using debit cards instead of cash. The money is transferred from their bank account to the store's bank account.

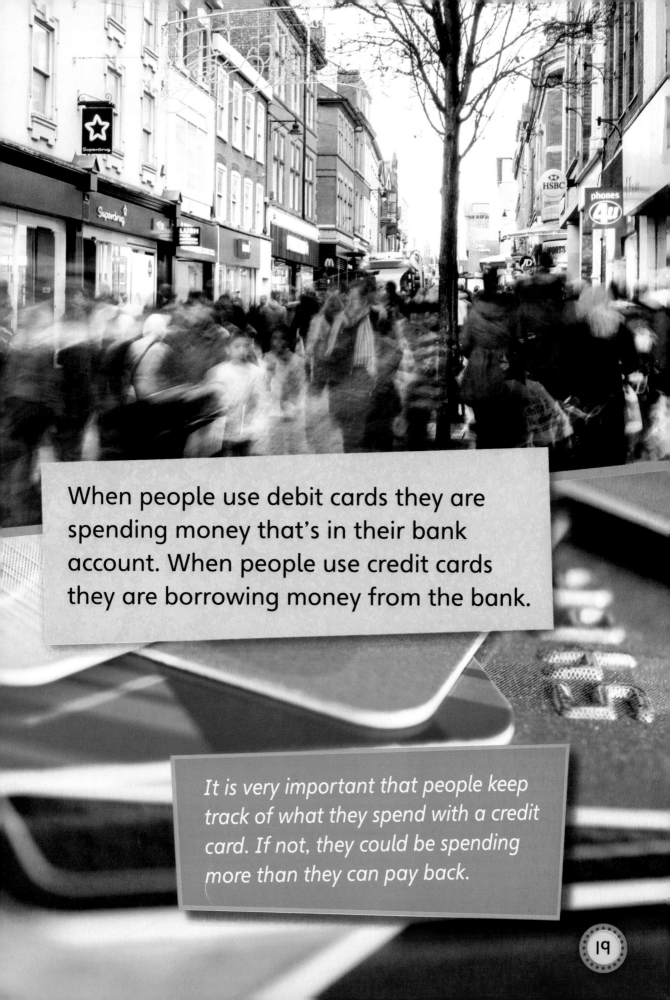

When people use debit cards they are spending money that's in their bank account. When people use credit cards they are borrowing money from the bank.

It is very important that people keep track of what they spend with a credit card. If not, they could be spending more than they can pay back.

How Much Is That Loaf of Bread?

The cost of everyday items depends on where you live.

This is what common items cost in different countries. What do these items cost where you live?

	Eggs (12)	Loaf of bread	Bananas (6)
India	$0.39	$0.28	$0.40
Hong Kong	$1.80	$0.23	$0.50
Russia	$3.39	$0.77	$0.62
United Kingdom	$5.28	$1.60	$1.57
Brazil	$0.84	$1.17	$0.25
Kuwait	$2.33	$1.06	$0.94
Belgium	$4.09	$1.92	$0.49

All figures in U.S. dollars (2015)

Did You Know?
Some people study how things are made, bought, and sold. They are called economists.

What Is GDP?

GDP (Gross Domestic Product) is the total value of goods and services a country produces in one year. Economists divide the GDP by the population of each country. This gives an estimate of the GDP per capita (per person).

	GDP per capita (2013) (U.S. dollars)
Norway	$100,819
United States of America	$53,142
United Kingdom	$41,787
Botswana	$7,315
Cambodia	$1,007
Burundi	$267

How Happy Is Your Country?

The fourth king of Bhutan believed that money was less important than happiness. Bhutan measures the Gross National Happiness of its citizens. The government measures things such as education and health to make sure people are happy.

A circus performer earns less than a surgeon. But if you love performing, this might be a perfect job for you.

What Do You Think?
Does happiness depend on how rich you are? A big salary might be good, but you might not like your job. A lower wage might be fine if you love your work.

Meet Some Young Entrepreneurs

An entrepreneur is a person who sets up a new business. Sometimes the person has an idea that no one else has thought of. It could be a new video game that everyone wants to play. It could be a useful tool to help people do their work. People with successful ideas can make lots of money!

These young entrepreneurs have all started their own businesses.

Fraser Doherty

Started business at age 14

Sells jam based on his grandma's recipe

Sean Belnick

Started business at age 14

Started with office chairs, now sells many products online

Moziah Bridges

Started business at age 9

Makes bow ties and sells them online

Brooke Martin

Started business at age 12

Invented a remote-controlled dog treat dispenser and phone app

Leanna Archer

Started business at age 11

Sells natural hair-care products

The Next Big Idea

Do you have lots of ideas? Do you work well on your own? Are you good at working with a team? Have you ever thought about starting your own company?

Pocket Money

You don't have to be an entrepreneur to earn money! Sometimes parents give their children money each week. A regular income is a great way to practice money skills such as budgeting.

Which of These Chores Do You Do?

sweep floor

wash dishes

water plants

take out garbage

rake leaves

shovel snow

weed garden

walk dog

What Do You Think?
Sometimes children get pocket money for no particular reason. Sometimes they must first do chores. Which makes more sense to you? Why?

Budgeting

What Is a Budget?

A budget is a plan. It helps you save and spend your money sensibly. If you know how much money you have, you can set up a budget.

Weekly Income and Expenses

INCOME	
Pocket money	$5.00
Dog-walking	$2.00
Total income	**$7.00**

EXPENSES	
Magazines	$3.00
Hamster food for Nigel	$2.00
Chocolate	$0.75
TOTAL EXPENSES	**$5.75**

Total income	$7.00
−Total expenses	−$5.75
AMOUNT LEFT TO SAVE	**$1.25**

Try to save $1.25 per week. It may not seem like much, but in one year you would have $65.00.

Families use budgets to decide how to spend their money. Housing and food are common items in family budgets.

Save It

Quiz
Are You a Spender or a Saver?

You have some money in your pocket. Do you spend it right away?

Yes **No**

You see something cool. Do you buy it?

Yes **No**

Is it hard to save your money?

Yes **No**

Did you answer yes to most questions? You are probably a spender, not a saver. It's fine to shop, but it's also good to save some money.

It is best to put your savings in a bank. A bank will pay interest on money in your account. By saving money, you can earn more!

Glossary

entrepreneur	person who starts and runs a business
fees	charges or payments
income	money earned or received
purchase	something you buy
salary	regular payment given to someone who works at a job
transaction	an instance of buying or selling something

Index

banks 10, 16, 17, 18, 19, 31
budgeting 26, 28–29
chores 27
coins 10–11, 12
credit cards 18–19
currency 8–9
debit cards 18–19

electronic transfers 17
entrepreneurs 24–25
paper money 14–15
pocket money 26–27
saving money 28, 29, 30–31
trade 6–9

Money Matters!

Why does money matter? Take a journey through the world of money, from trading cattle to making electronic transfers. Who were the first people to use money and how do we use money today?

PEARSON

ISBN-13: 978-0-328-83281-1
ISBN-10:   0-328-83281-2

9 780328 832811

90000 >